I Love Our Earth

Bill Martin Jr and Michael Sampson
Photographs by Dan Lipow

Charlesbridge

For Kelley Fincher—B. M.

For Grete Sampson—M. S.

To my daughter Hannah:
I look forward to sharing and exploring the whole wonderful world with you—D. L.

Text copyright © 2006 by Bill Martin Jr and Michael Sampson
Photographs copyright © 2006 by Dan Lipow
All rights reserved, including the right of reproduction in whole or in part in any form. Charlesbridge and colophon are registered trademarks of Charlesbridge Publishing, Inc.

Published by Charlesbridge, 85 Main Street, Watertown, MA 02472
(617) 926-0329 ● www.charlesbridge.com

Library of Congress Cataloging-in-Publication Data
Martin, Bill, 1916-2004
    I love our Earth / Bill Martin, Jr., and Michael Sampson ; photographs by
Dan Lipow.
        p. cm.
    ISBN-13: 978-1-58089-106-6 (reinforced for library use)
    ISBN-10: 1-58089-106-3 (reinforced for library use)
1. Earth—Juvenile literature. I. Sampson, Michael R. II. Lipow, Dan, ill. III. Title.
QB631.4.M368 2006
525—dc22   2005006008

Printed in Thailand
(hc) 10 9 8 7 6 5 4 3 2 1

Type set in Ingone, designed by Robert Schenk, Ingrimayne Type
Color separations by Chroma Graphics, Singapore
Printed and bound by Imago
Production supervision by Brian G. Walker
Designed by Susan Mallory Sherman

E
MAR

I love our Earth . . .

where green grasses ripple,

and gray mountains
rise,

where blue oceans
curl,

and brown deserts
swirl.

I love our Earth . . .

for wet forests
that drip,

and dry winds
that drift,

for cool mosses
that grow,

and warm sunsets
that glow.

I love our Earth . . .

when summer stars
flicker,

and autumn leaves
flame,

when winter flakes
blow,

and spring blossoms
show.

I love our Earth!